A Man of Emails

Also by Michael Byrne and published by Ginninderra Press
Estuary at Dusk
Southbound
New & Selected Poems
On Common Water (editor)
Indigo Book of Australian Prose Poems (editor)

Michael Byrne

A Man of Emails

Acknowledgements

Some of these poems first appeared, sometimes in a different form, in *Bipolar Poetry*, *Quadrant*, *The Best Australian Poetry* 2009 (University of Queensland Press), *The Canberra Times* and *Treci Trg* (Serbia).

Some of the poems have been read on the radio program *Soundprint* (2XX).

Thanks must go to Geoff Page and John Foulcher for their assistance with the drafting of poems in this book.

The first stanza of 'Heat' paraphrases the first verse of a song by The Doors called 'Light My Fire'. Acknowledgement is made to the songwriter Robby Krieger.

A Man of Emails
ISBN 978 1 74027 603 0
Copyright © text Michael Byrne 2010

First published 2010
Reprinted 2015

GINNINDERRA PRESS
PO Box 3461 Port Adelaide SA 5015
www.ginninderrapress.com.au

Contents

Inbox	7
Heat	9
My First Lithium	10
The Similes and Metaphors Alone	11
Life with Your Very First Set of Wheels	12
Sunday	13
Poem for Craig Nicholls	14
Sent Items	15
Love	17
Vietnam	18
Down the Line	19
An Oppressive Summer Storm	21
The Cockatoo	23
A Brisk and Pleasant Walk after Rain	25
Night Sounds	26
The Virus I Caught from the Television	27
Aquatics	29
Codral	37
The Catwalk	38

Inbox

Heat

You think I would be untrue,
you think I would be a liar,
if I were to say to you
that your swimming pool is on fire.

But it actually and factually is.
In flames like a burning pyre,
incandescent like a Roman candle,
your swimming pool is on fire.

For your beautiful daughter is bathing.
Her breasts and legs I admire.
As long as she is burning within it,
your swimming pool is on fire!

My First Lithium

I was twenty-one, and high and mighty.
I stomped to my psychiatrist, angry.

I took a seat, felt better, turned mellow.
I went in, happy as a child in snow.

Then I asked him for an arm wrestle,
got turned down. I began to whistle

and asked the man where he went to school
as if it mattered, where there were rules

and always someone aberrant to break them.
I had become much more interesting again.

I sang happy songs to a portrait, a windowsill.
He turfed me out, gave me water and a bitter pill

to swallow, like the diagnosis, a habit I had to keep.
Something I never had before, but needed, like sleep.

The Similes and Metaphors Alone

The sky above is a swarm of bees
while overgrown vegetables are trees.
My two hands open like flowers,
lungs are clocks to measure the hours.
My pills are stones thrown into the ocean,
my hair is a wave about to break,
grey shadow covers my face like lotion,
my pen is poised like a striking snake.

Books are faces that never change.
My clock sounds like a rhythmic clap.
Stalagmites are a mountain range.
The glass half empty a steel trap.
Night illuminates like a bright idea.
A finished poem is a finished beer.

Life with Your Very First Set of Wheels

    A kid happily hoons down a hill,
brakes and slides. It reminds me
        of my very first set of wheels, the thrill.
Cruising through the suburbs, free,
        to the hallowed house of a friend.
The bright blue and white, the cool wind,
        everything was alive and fresh and new,
icy poles never better. Love was true

and innocent. Down steep and hard hills we went
        and up them, with lactic acid filling legs
but never stopping. Bunny hops on cement,
        throwing water bombs at cars, laughing with skegs
and just generally being a pesky pest.
        Life with your very first set of wheels is best.

Sunday

Sunday is for throwing a lasso
of random words to friends,
for tying up, not discarding,
any loose or frayed ends.

Sunday is for joyous dancing
to blithe songs with caffeine
that make you high, like clear blue sky,
like pseudoephedrine.

And Sunday is the perfect day
for lawnmowers that snarl,
for curtly combing hair straight
that will soon after curl.

Sunday is for sweat that seeds
your weathered and wan face
and clumped and slumped cotton clothes
tossed across the place.

This hot and humid Sunday moves
at the pace of a snail,
while folded, curdled curtains swell
with blowing air like sails.

While slackly slumped near the fan
or close to sleep in bed,
books of verse whisper secrets
you only hear when read.

Poem for Craig Nicholls

(Lead singer of The Vines, Craig Nicholls, was recently diagnosed with Asperger's syndrome.)

How strange the way things have changed and evolved,
how doing nothing gets a problem solved
and how something gets diagnosed
after opinions are imposed
about your propensity for being irate
and wild and erratic and petulant,
you have to break down life to what you want
for the sake of your band and fans and your own fate.

You thrash and flail with your guitar
and burn your barren voice out with screams
and burn yourself out like a fallen star
and nothing for you is what it seems,
ablaze under tempestuous skies
with swinging guitar and upturned eyes.

Sent Items

Love

love builds towers out of gold
love is the pot at the end of the rainbow
love is the perfect state of trust and unity
try having life without love
i am constantly learning about it
love will make enemies out of your friends
love will make sane men insane and vice versa
love climbs the mountain and walks back down

Vietnam

Vietnam did my Dad some harm
all those brave and courageous soldiers
running through the thick and lush jungle
paupers and puppets in a piss weak war
Dad won the lottery of lotteries
by getting conscripted to go
Dad took some lovely photographs
and got shot at in an armoured car

Down the Line

An Oppressive Summer Storm

Heavy, dense, swelling clouds
        hang over the urban landscape.
The sky has been fermenting.

Cars rev down Southern Cross Drive,
        a boy stamps on his skateboard
and heads off, trees shake in the wind.

Some green traffic lights glow brightly.
        I stroll across a small zebra crossing.
A car rolls, then stops politely.

A nearby bus groans, lurches and hisses.
        The air is humid and dank and muggy.
A tiny pee-wee flits below a sky

that is a frothing, curdled white;
        with an overlapping darker hue
that is like smudged charcoal.

A schoolboy peddles past me,
        anxious to get indoors – below a roof,
not a sky that threatens to burst.

I cross some streets, cars curve off.
        I stroll down the damp path
beside the shrivelled weeds.

The first evanescent drop I feel
        splashes on my nose, then more
drops fire down, then rain thickens.

I snatch my black raincoat
        from my bag, fasten the buttons,
tie the hood in a ramshackle knot.

My shoes squelch and the rain thickens still.
        This awkward and oppressive limbo
between the haven of my house and hell.

Now hailstones hammer on my hood.
        The white beads make a popping sound
like popcorn shooting inside a microwave.

I dip my heavy, hail-shotten head
        as I walk up this tiring, battered hill;
as if fervently immersed in prayer,

then I leave the violent atmosphere
        to exhaust itself, through sheer spent force,
let nature run its due and true course.

The Cockatoo

        With seeming ease, a white cockatoo
lands on our ochre birdbath.
        His scalloped plumage is replicated

in the motionless clouds
        which hang above me
on this cooling afternoon.

        The cockatoo sports a majestic mohawk
as if pummelled with pomade
        if not for the end which sticks up

like an untucked tag.
        While he is dipping his head
a currawong signals his intent

        by hopping onto a light near the birdbath.
Then swoops. A second currawong swoops
        then a third. Not deterred, the white bird

dips and rises, dips and rises
        before another currawong waiting
swoops him too. Still the cockatoo

        comes back, drinks and comes up.
Then the cockatoo flies off
        as a currawong takes his turn.

A couple of other currawongs drink as well.
        Then the birdbath is left alone.
The crafty cockatoo comes back and drinks

       from the small pool of water.
A friend joins him and they work the ochre birdbath,
       dipping and rising, dipping and rising,

talons firmly clamped to a rim of stone.
       Then they fly off, their white wings
flapping through the tepid air.

       The spectacle for today is over.
A sort of strange, silent documentary
       where the bird I liked the most

got the last laugh. My cigarette is dying
       in an ashtray. Smoke is lingering,
like persistent things with wings.

A Brisk and Pleasant Walk after Rain

        I near a small pool of water
     with a plastic bag floating on it
like a solitary yacht.
        The water thins out under an overpass
            like the waning tail of spermatozoa.

        Two people ahead walk with bright jackets
     and a black dog bounding along,
happy and hyperactive.
        I veer off to walk at the fringe
            of an oval, bypassing the bench

        with its beads of moisture
     and sit on a hard, damp log.
A car slices steam from a road.
        I head back along the same track.
            I pass a jogger, straining yet headstrong.

        Then I near a terse teenager
     in a go-kart. He sways towards me.
I meet his eye, and he veers off. I smile.
        Satisfied with it all, I pass his associates
            and stroll up the hill to my house.

        Then I stop and stare at a currawong,
     hunched and bunched over a street light.
Alone and sombre, still as he is silent,
        with yellow patchwork eyes. He stares out
            as the sun puts a gloss on the world.

Night Sounds

Almost every night, the man next door
throws away beer bottles, you can hear

the rattle and clang as he disposes of them.
Their little dog yaps away at whatever.

Last week, I heard a rustle, close,
in our bushes and flicked on my light.

I felt wary and woke Dad. He laboured
to unlock our screen door for a while,

then we set ourselves to go outside.
Dad flicked three switches, and the yard

was lit in half-light. I felt the cool, hard ground
under my feet. Dad groped for a torch in the shed,

then probed some nearby trees. He clutched
at a spider web that clung to his face,

then removed it. We went round the side,
sifting through bushes. Nothing. Out the front,

the same empty silence. Dad headed
to our musty and dusty garage

where he grabbed his old army machete.
Around the side again, again the same situation.

Dad says he keeps the side gate locked
and it's too high for someone to scale.

So that is that. Possibly a cat.
An unsolved mystery, like a woman.

The Virus I Caught from the Television

        Once upon a time, my television
had a virus. It slithered out of the windows
        of a glass house, lit a fire in the loins,
chewed the fat of people on the screen,
        spread its germs, watched a president sweat.

I felt bad vibrations, frantic frustrations,
        it was a sad situation. I got it, laughed at lies,
went to bed, until the thoughts I was thinking
        turned sour in an hour and I cowered
in a hapless hospital for the helpless.

        It left a bitter taste in my mouth,
while beer tasted like lolly water. I lost
        someone too in the process, the excess,
the flaming trees. Logic was laughter.
        I breathed daft punk but not skunk.

I nearly lost myself to the virus – this strain
        turned ugly, it came from the mouth
of a ham who did not give a damn.
        I swam in a dram before the second chapter,
the second chance, the second coming,

        the fixed plumbing, the cheerful humming,
not succumbing to the persisting symptoms.
        Not grumbling but numbly fumbling
with a pen leaking happy sentiment.
        Experience not to my detriment.

Eventually my television got better.
>It kicked the habit of hostility and got back
to doing what it does blessed. It still
>gets symptoms of reference but does not hurt me.
If it gets confused I just treat it by referring to books.

Aquatics

1

A bodyboard is like a nose –
break it and it hurts,

naked to the pounding fists
of rock or reef.

Like a nose it has contour, shape,
people perform surgery on both,

both yield to some degree.
You cannot ride a nose, though,

but nostrils are like channels –
they both gush spray.

Digging a rail into a wave
is like hooking a nose into a smell –

they are all different,
some pristine, others ordinary.

Exiting a tube
is like breathing fresh oxygen, again.

A nose cannot float
but can be immersed in water.

Both hate it. It proves difficult
to lose a nose.

Both are used for the perception
of the senses. You become attached to both.

2

Mavericks. Light rain slants and falls
on surfers with balls surfing bowls.

A long and freezing paddle out.
Sharky. The water dark and murky.

Just latching onto a wave is hard.
And making the drop as the lip pours,

plenty of froth to sink under
if not keen to steal its thunder.

Make a blunder at this water wonder
and you could be rendered return to sender.

Death is a possibility. The horror of hold-downs.
No fancy moves, just bottom turns and grooves.

Just fearsome, awesome mountains
of water. Waves to end all waves.

3

I busted a barrel roll today.
Launching with the lip,

the world swung out of focus
and swung back in. I landed it,

dumbfounded – it was my first one.
But I tweaked it too slow

to latch onto the surging wave
rolling to the rocks.

Still, it was good.
Moves are mastery

of the ocean, what you remember.
Cutbacks are commonplace, for me,

I slice waves in my sleep.
Once I did an aerial at Airports –

it was almost an accident.
I did another at Pacific Palms.

I was speeding along
to an oncoming section,

I launched
and held my board above my head,

then landed. It was an epiphany.
Any moves are mastery.

Moves are beads,
strung onto the necklace of a surf.

4

I walk down a tarred road, to take
one last sentimental look at the surf

in the waning afternoon sun.
Onshore wind pummels my face

as I arrive, and watch clumsy surf
tripping over itself, then falling.

Drunken, it gropes and ropes around
the clenched fists of the rocks.

How quickly the wind has smothered
it all. This morning, the offshore breeze

put its hand through the hair of waves.
Now white caps, like seagull droppings.

How fickle the ocean can be.
How the surf changes, like seasons.

5

Pipeline. The name says it all.
Some men will stand while others fall.

They paddle fast to the shoulder,
duck dive below tumbling white water,

sit among hardened and sullen locals,
waiting calmly for a warping wave.

They see the gleaming scales of walls
below the spray blown back like hair,

watch perfect play-frame peaks
funnelling in cylindrical glory,

then spitting and hissing viciously.
The spray alone can knock you off.

One person a year dies from surfing Pipe.
You can drop off without even dropping in.

6

I surfed the shorebreak at Plantation
today. Big shrivelled lumps of swell

coming through. Rough, with backwash.
The surf was choppy and sloppy

like wavy water being panned for gold.
I got a couple of reasonable walls.

I pulled into a close-out, the savage surf
grabbed me in a headlock and flung me

to the sand. The final wave was four foot.
A steep drop. I pulled in, got wrecked.

I liked the two close-outs best of all.
Ephemeral. A world within a world.

7

There will always be dangerous days.
I have lived through uneasy situations.

Big bombs breaking over my head,
being caught up in the wrathful turbulence,

being sucked into nowhere like a sweet,
licked and sucked by tongues of waves,

pulling into angry, angry close-outs
that had no interest in my survival,

getting on the bad side
of other bothered board riders,

cuts from reefs with no sympathy.
You're never safer than when you're on land.

8

For me, surfing will always be
about the simple pleasures.

Rising lazily over a burnished mound
of hardened and smooth liquid slate,

the jouissance of the temperature adjustment
as your body conforms to the chill,

spying four foot offshore sets making a pilgrimage
to the shore like beached and parched whales,

surviving a six-foot close-out bomb
breaking on your head with a vengeance,

or catching a tiny shoot in
and arriving at the shore.

Codral

Six dry tablets
washed down with coffee

and I'm there
momentarily, temporarily,

my limbs blushing,
my breathing subdued,

taken to a place,
a feeling, a thought

where a kite flails and dips
in a clear blue sky,

where fingers dance like butterflies
over a fretboard.

The Catwalk

I look through the large, clear frames
of the library window. The compacted pavers
of the adjacent embankment become a strange catwalk
where elegant, suave models are random humans;
young, lithe women – with or without cigarettes
or friends. Some carry green drooping bags,
all have demeanours. They casually stroll
into this bipolar weather – alternating
moods of sunshine and cold, harsh sleet
with constant, fierce, leaf-tossing wind
sending trees and bushes into spasms
as clouds drag and sag across the sun.
Inside the library, a loud baby howls,
a woman nearby flicks through a paper
and men behind me talk in hushed voices.
Outside, young women stroll a strange catwalk.
Blue clouds spread like an ink blot on a perfect dress,
captured by the flickering flash photography of lightning.

Michael Byrne was born in Sydney in 1978. A year later, he moved to Tuross Head on the New South Wales South Coast. He came to live in Canberra in 1987. He holds an Arts degree from the Australian National University and a Masters in Journalism from the University of Wollongong. He has worked in community journalism and as a reviewer, anthologist and freelance poetry tutor.

www.ingramcontent.com/pod-product-compliance
Lightning Source LLC
Chambersburg PA
CBHW062207100526
44589CB00014B/1990